Who .

Pa

Who Was
Paul Revere?

By Roberta Edwards
Illustrated by John O'Brien

Grosset & Dunlap
An Imprint of Penguin Group (USA) Inc.

For my daughter Tess—JO

GROSSET & DUNLAP
Published by the Penguin Group
Penguin Group (USA) Inc., 375 Hudson Street, New York, New York 10014, USA
Penguin Group (Canada), 90 Eglinton Avenue East, Suite 700,
Toronto, Ontario M4P 2Y3, Canada (a division of Pearson Penguin Canada Inc.)
Penguin Books Ltd., 80 Strand, London WC2R 0RL, England
Penguin Group Ireland, 25 St. Stephen's Green, Dublin 2, Ireland
(a division of Penguin Books Ltd.)
Penguin Group (Australia), 250 Camberwell Road, Camberwell, Victoria 3124, Australia
(a division of Pearson Australia Group Pty. Ltd.)
Penguin Books India Pvt. Ltd., 11 Community Centre,
Panchsheel Park, New Delhi—110 017, India
Penguin Group (NZ), 67 Apollo Drive, Rosedale, Auckland 0632, New Zealand
(a division of Pearson New Zealand Ltd.)
Penguin Books (South Africa) (Pty.) Ltd., 24 Sturdee Avenue,
Rosebank, Johannesburg 2196, South Africa

Penguin Books Ltd., Registered Offices:
80 Strand, London WC2R 0RL, England

Text copyright © 2011 by Penguin Group (USA) Inc. Interior illustrations copyright
© 2011 by John O'Brien. Cover illustration copyright © 2011 by Nancy Harrison.
All rights reserved. Published by Grosset & Dunlap, a division of
Penguin Young Readers Group, 345 Hudson Street, New York, New York 10014.
GROSSET & DUNLAP is a trademark of Penguin Group (USA) Inc.
Printed in the U.S.A.

Library of Congress Control Number: 2011011885

ISBN 978-0-448-45715-4   10 9 8 7 6 5 4 3 2 1

Contents

Who Was
Paul Revere?

Paul Revere was a clever boy. He was also a boy who liked having money in his pocket. At fifteen, he came up with a smart idea for a business.

Near his family's home in Boston, Massachusetts, was Old North Church. It was sometimes called Eight Bell Church because of

its eight huge brass bells. The smallest one weighed more than six hundred pounds. The largest weighed more than fifteen hundred pounds. Bell ringers pulled ropes on the bells to move them. Each bell made a different chime; all together, the ringing bells sounded beautiful. To this day they are considered the best bells in Boston.

The bells weren't just rung on Sunday mornings. If there was a fire, they were rung. When somebody died, the bells rang out the number of the person's age. The bells were rung for many reasons.

Paul figured that the church might need extra bell ringers. And he was right. The church agreed to pay Paul and six friends three shillings a week for their services. Shillings were British coins made from silver. At that time, everyone in Massachusetts used British money. That's because the colony belonged to Great Britain. It was one of thirteen British colonies in America.

Paul wanted to make sure that all the bell ringers did their fair share of work. So he wrote up a contract. It described what the boys had to do as bell ringers. It said that every three months a different boy would hand out the money. New members could only join if everyone in the group voted them in. Paul also wrote that no member would ever "begg" for money. The members of the

bell-ringing business *worked* for their money.

Today, the contract is in the museum of Old North Church. It is neatly written. Paul's handwriting is quite fancy.

The contract says much about Paul Revere. He was a boy who believed in fairness. He didn't care about being the boss. The boys would take turns being in charge of the money. The group, not Paul alone, would make decisions. This was an important idea at that time, especially in Boston. Many people resented how powerful the king of England was. Why should one man control thousands of people living far away in the thirteen colonies?

Bell ringing was also just the right business for Paul Revere. In the eighteenth century, telephones, televisions, and computers were all far in the future. Bell ringing signaled big news. The people of Boston would flock to churches to find out what was going on.

Paul liked being at the center of things. And throughout his life, that's where you could usually find him. By the 1770s, many Americans were ready to break away from England and start a brand-new country. Paul Revere was one of them. He was not a leader of the American Revolution like George Washington or John Adams. But he spread the news about the Revolution.

In some way, he was a bell ringer all his life.

SPELLING IN THE 1700S

IN THE CONTRACT THAT PAUL REVERE WROTE FOR HIS BELL-RINGING BUSINESS, HE SPELLED *BEG* WITH TWO *G*S, LIKE THIS: *BEGG*. THAT WASN'T CONSIDERED A MISTAKE BACK IN THE 1700S. THERE WERE NOT STRICT RULES FOR SPELLING THE WAY THERE ARE TODAY. IN FACT, THE FIRST AMERICAN DICTIONARY WAS NOT PUBLISHED UNTIL 1806 BY NOAH WEBSTER.

NOAH WEBSTER

WEBSTER SPENT TWENTY YEARS WORKING ON THE FIRST EDITION OF HIS DICTIONARY.

IT LISTED THE SPELLINGS OF WORDS AS WELL AS THEIR MEANINGS. HE WANTED TO MAKE SPELLING SIMPLER.

WEBSTER ALSO WANTED AMERICAN SPELLING TO BREAK AWAY FROM BRITISH SPELLING. AFTER ALL, THE UNITED STATES WAS NO LONGER PART OF ENGLAND. SO WHY SHOULD AMERICANS KEEP FOLLOWING BRITISH SPELLING RULES? HE DROPPED THE *K* IN WORDS LIKE *PUBLIC*. IN WORDS LIKE *HUMOUR* AND *HONOUR*, THE *OU* WAS SHORTENED TO *O* SO THEY WERE SPELLED *HUMOR* AND *HONOR*. MANY OF WEBSTER'S SPELLING RULES STUCK. BUT SOME DID NOT. HE THOUGHT *TONGUE* SHOULD BE SPELLED "TUNG" AND *WOMEN* SHOULD BE SPELLED "WIMMIN."

Chapter 1
Boston Boy

In the last week of 1734, Paul Revere was born in the town of Boston. He was the first boy in the family. His older sister, Deborah, was about three years older than Paul. His mother, who was also named Deborah, was from Boston. Her family had come to America about one hundred years earlier. After Paul, Deborah had seven more children, but two died when they were still babies.

Paul's father was from France. His name was Apollos Rivoire. (say: APP-all-us RIV-war.) When he was only thirteen, he came to America all by himself. Apollos's family sent him, hoping he would have a better life than he could in France. The ship landed in Boston, which became his

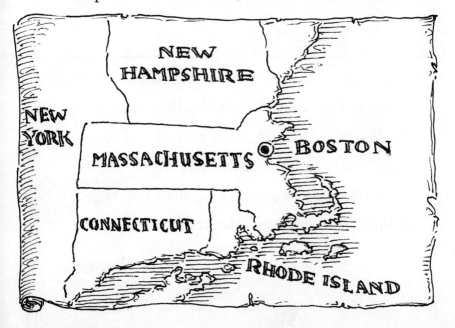

new home. He arrived knowing barely a word of
English. But soon Paul's father learned a trade.
He became a silversmith, a really good one. In
time, Paul's father opened his own
shop. He made some very beautiful
things. Two small gold buttons with a

beautiful flower pattern show his skill and talent.

Because so many people had trouble pronouncing his name, Paul's father decided to change it. He wanted a name that sounded more American. So Apollos Rivoire became Paul Revere.

The Reveres lived in a small house on Fish Street. It was close to the harbor. There were only about thirteen thousand people living in Boston when Paul was a child. No house was more than a few streets from water.

Paul grew up watching ships arrive from

England bringing tea, furniture, and other goods for people in the colonies. Ships made the return trip to Europe bringing things from America—timber, rice, cotton, and tobacco. Besides the big trading ships, hundreds of small boats went out every day fishing for cod, lobsters, and oysters.

Paul was bright and full of energy. He had dark hair and brown eyes like his father. He loved swimming, riding horses, and playing with his friends.

ALPHABET
VOWELS
PHONICS
LORD'S PRAYER

HORNBOOK

As a small boy, Paul went to a school where strict, old women taught boys and girls the alphabet. Students used hornbooks, small wooden paddles covered with a clear sheet of animal horn. A lesson would be slipped under the horn so it wouldn't get dirty. (Children who made mistakes in their lessons were bopped on the head with a stick.)

At age seven, Paul was sent to North Writing School. In Boston, there were two kinds of public schools. Both were just for boys. Grammar schools prepared students for colleges such as Harvard and Yale. After that, they would begin careers as lawyers, doctors, and ministers. Writing schools were for middle-class boys like Paul who would become craftsmen. There, he learned math and good penmanship.

Paul's most important teacher was his father.

He taught Paul to be a silversmith. The shop may have been in a separate little building next to their house. As an apprentice, or beginner, Paul worked beside his father every day. At first, he could only do simple jobs. He swept the floor, making sure he brushed up all the silver dust so it could be reused. He put more coal in the furnace that melted down the silver. Learning how to work silver was difficult. It cracked easily. It took many years to become a master silversmith.

The work was dangerous, too. Furnaces melted blocks of silver at temperatures reaching two thousand degrees. The melted silver was poured into molds and left to harden. If an apprentice was not careful, he could end up badly burned.

A flat, thin piece of silver was placed on a
metal block called an anvil and hammered into
simple things like spoons and knives. Early on,
Paul learned to hammer out dents in bowls and
plates. He learned to make silver thimbles. He
repaired the hinges on tankards. Tankards were
large mugs that came with hinged lids. Paul's
training probably lasted about seven years.

SILVERSMITH SHOP

A. SILVER, OFTEN FROM COINS, IS MELTED ON
   A HOT FURNACE FUELED BY COAL AND
   BELLOWS.

B. THE MOLTEN SILVER IS POURED INTO MOLDS
   CALLED CRUCIBLES.

C. WHEN COOLED, THEY PRODUCE INGOTS.

D. THE INGOTS ARE POUNDED FLAT AND

E. THEN SKILLFULLY HAMMERED ON AN ANVIL
   INTO PLATES, BOWLS, GOBLETS, AND OTHER
   SILVERWARE.

F. FINALLY THE PIECES ARE ENGRAVED OR
   DECORATED IN A VARIETY OF WAYS.

The silver pieces made by the Reveres were simple but graceful. Sometimes a fancy tray or bowl might be decorated with silver shells or bunches of grapes. Sometimes they were engraved. That means a design was scratched into the surface of the silver. Paul became an expert at using a sharp engraving tool called a burin. The last step was to take a cloth and polish the piece of silver until its surface shone like a mirror!

When Paul was only nineteen, his father died. Now Paul had to run the silver shop with help from his younger brother Tom. (His brother John decided to become a tailor.) After a year or so, however, Paul made a big change in his life. He wanted to leave Boston. Perhaps he had grown tired of the silver business. Perhaps he wanted to have an adventure.

Paul left his brother in charge of the shop and went off to be a soldier.

Chapter 2
Colonial Soldier

The thirteen colonies that belonged to
England stretched along the Atlantic coast as far
south as Georgia.

By the mid-1700s there were about two million colonists living on what amounted to more than 322 thousand square miles of land.

The king of England, however, wanted more land.

KING GEORGE III OF ENGLAND

He had his eye on what is now part of Canada. He also wanted land in the Ohio River Valley and by the mouth of the Mississippi River. The problem was that the king of France already had settlements in these areas. And he was not about to give them up.

So England and France went to war. The war became known as the French and Indian War because many Native American tribes sided with France. It lasted a long time—from 1754 to 1763.

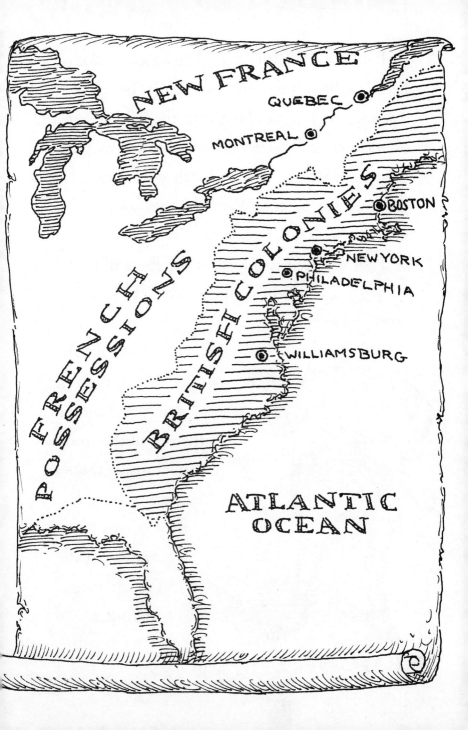

Even though Paul was an American colonist, he was a British citizen. So when he became a soldier, he fought along with the British army. Soldiers from England wore a uniform with a bright red jacket. That's why they were called redcoats. Colonial soldiers like Paul wore a uniform with a dark blue jacket.

Paul was sent to a fort on the shore of Lake George in upstate New York. The French troops were nearby. All through the summer, Paul and the rest of the troops remained inside the fort. They were waiting for their enemy to strike. But the French were waiting, too.

REDCOAT

They expected the British to fire the first shot. Finally, in November, Paul went home to Boston. (The battle did eventually start, and the British won it.)

GEORGE WASHINGTON

George Washington was another colonial soldier who fought for the British in the French and Indian War. He helped build around eighty forts. Unlike Paul Revere, he took part in battles. George Washington learned a lot about both winning and losing. The French and Indian War was a training ground for him. Thirteen years later, General George Washington led colonial troops to victory in the American Revolution.

THE FUR TRADE

IT SEEMS SILLY TO SAY THAT A WAR WAS FOUGHT OVER BEAVERS. BUT THAT'S PARTLY TRUE IN THE CASE OF THE FRENCH AND INDIAN WAR.

IN THE 1700S, BEAVER WAS THE MOST EXPENSIVE FUR. RICH MEN IN EUROPE ALL WANTED HATS MADE OF BEAVER FUR. THERE WERE PLENTY OF BEAVERS LIVING IN THE LANDS THAT FRANCE CONTROLLED IN AMERICA. THE FRENCH MADE A FORTUNE BRINGING BEAVER SKINS, OR PELTS, BACK TO EUROPE. ENGLAND WANTED TO TAKE OVER THE FUR TRADE. THE WAY TO DO IT WAS TO TAKE OVER THE LAND THAT THE FRENCH CONTROLLED.

THE FUR TRADE LASTED UNTIL AROUND 1840. BY THEN, THERE WEREN'T MANY BEAVERS LEFT IN AMERICA. THEY HAD BEEN OVERHUNTED. TOWNS

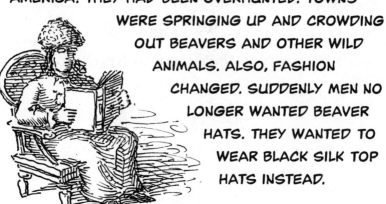

WERE SPRINGING UP AND CROWDING OUT BEAVERS AND OTHER WILD ANIMALS. ALSO, FASHION CHANGED. SUDDENLY MEN NO LONGER WANTED BEAVER HATS. THEY WANTED TO WEAR BLACK SILK TOP HATS INSTEAD.

Chapter 3
Family Life

Paul returned to Boston and his life as a silversmith. He wanted a family of his own now, and it didn't take him long to find a good wife. In August of 1757 he married Sara Orne. He called her Sary. Not much is known about her.

The young couple lived in the house where Paul had grown up. His mother still lived there, too; in fact, she lived with her son and his family until she died. However, now she paid rent to Paul. (This was the custom at the time.)

Paul and Sary's first child, a little girl named Deborah, was born in 1758. Every two years,

Sary had another child. Paul called them his "little lambs." By 1773, she'd given birth to eight children, but three died young. In the late 1700s, babies and young children often didn't live long. There were no medicines to cure fevers.

Sometimes outbreaks of a deadly disease called smallpox spread through Boston. Horrible sores broke out on a person's face and body. If smallpox didn't kill you, it left you scarred for life.

As for Sary, she fell sick and died not long after her last baby was born. The baby, Isanna, survived a little longer, then died, too. It was a hard time for Paul. He had a large family. His mother was growing older. He needed a wife to care for the children. He met Rachel Walker and, in less than a year, they were married. Paul and Rachel were very happy together. She was clever like Paul. And dark-haired, too. In a poem he wrote for her, he said that she was "the fair one who is closest to my heart." They had eight more children. Three of Rachel's babies died young, too. (Out of sixteen children, five were still alive when Paul died in 1818.)

Paul worked hard. He made whatever a customer wanted. Once, he made a silver chain for a pet squirrel. Another time,

RACHEL WALKER he made a

silver whistle for a child. He made lovely coffeepots, teapots, sugar bowls, and creamers. Today, pieces of silver by Paul Revere are in the finest museums in the United States.

Of course, he didn't only make fancy things for the rich people of Boston. In the 1760s, the city went through hard times. Shops were closing. A bank failed. Not nearly as many people could afford costly silver items. So what did Paul Revere do? He made buckles, eyeglass frames, and surgical tools. From iron he made keys, hooks, and locks. He learned to make copper engravings. With a burin, he could engrave a portrait or a scene onto a copper plate. Once the plate was inked, the image could be printed on paper. Was Paul Revere an artist? No. In fact, he was not very good at drawing. His engravings were copies of artists' work.

He even taught himself to make false teeth! This was a smart move. In colonial times, people suffered terribly from rotten teeth. One visitor from Sweden said that most young colonial girls he saw were missing half their teeth.

Paul made false teeth from the tusks of hippos. He printed ads that said his false teeth looked good. They were also comfortable to wear and "of real Use in Speaking and Eating."

He was hardworking and smart. But he also liked the company of friends. After work, he often headed to the nearest tavern. It was called the Green Dragon Tavern. A dragon hammered out of copper hung from a pole over the door. Taverns often had signs that explained their names. At the Green Dragon, Paul liked to play card games and backgammon. He enjoyed talking about politics with friends.

THE GREEN DRAGON TAVERN

He was a joiner. He became a member of quite a few men's groups. One held its meetings at the Green Dragon Tavern. Another met above a printing shop. The group was called the Long Room Club. Many men who became leaders of the American Revolution belonged to this club. A beer maker named Sam Adams was a member. So was John Hancock, who was one of the richest men in Boston. Most of the men had gone to Harvard, but they welcomed Paul. They admired his good sense and his energy.

At meetings of the Long Room Club, there was a lot of angry talk about taxes. Colonists had no say in what taxes they had to pay. The government in England decided their taxes. Was that fair? Not in the minds of the Long Room Club members. It had to stop!

TAVERNS

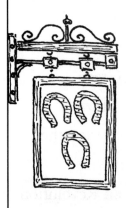

BOSTON HAD LOTS OF TAVERNS. IN 1740, THERE WERE MORE THAN THIRTY. THEY HAD INTERESTING NAMES SUCH AS NOAH'S ARK, BUNCH OF GRAPES, AND THREE HORSESHOES. FOR PEOPLE WHO COULDN'T READ, A PICTURE SIGN OVER THE DOOR (FOR EXAMPLE, A SIGN WITH THREE HORSESHOES) SHOWED THE TAVERN'S NAME. MANY TAVERNS IN THE COLONIES WERE CALLED THE "BLACK HORSE." THE NAME AND SIGN (SHOWING A BLACK HORSE, OF COURSE) TOLD TRAVELERS THAT THE TAVERN HAD ROOMS FOR THE NIGHT AS WELL AS STABLES FOR HORSES. IN BOSTON, THERE WAS A BLACK HORSE, A WHITE HORSE, AND A RED HORSE TAVERN.

IN PAUL'S TIME, TAVERNS WERE NOT JUST PLACES WHERE YOU'D GO TO EAT AND DRINK AND GOSSIP. TAVERNS WERE A CENTER OF TOWN LIFE. THERE WERE NO POST OFFICES YET. SO MAIL CARRIERS WOULD DROP OFF LETTERS AT TAVERNS. PEOPLE WHO LIVED NEARBY WOULD STOP IN AND CHECK FOR MAIL.

TAVERNS HELD LECTURES. THEY ALSO ACTED AS LIBRARIES, WITH BOOKS AND NEWSPAPERS FOR CUSTOMERS TO BORROW.

MOST IMPORTANT OF ALL, TAVERNS WERE LIKE TOWN HALLS. PEOPLE CAME TO TAVERNS TO DISCUSS IMPORTANT EVENTS OF THE DAY. POLITICAL LEADERS GATHERED AT TAVERNS LIKE THE GREEN DRAGON. THEY HOPED TO CONVINCE THE PEOPLE OF BOSTON THAT IT WAS TIME TO CUT FREE FROM ENGLAND.

Chapter 4
Taxes, Taxes, and More Taxes

The British won the French and Indian War. King George III now owned a lot more land in America. But the nine-year war had cost a lot of money. Also, now the king had to send hundreds of British soldiers to America to keep control of the new land. It cost a lot of money to house and feed a big army. England was in debt, big time.

The war had been fought in America. So why shouldn't colonists in America help pay for it through new taxes? At least, that's what Parliament thought. (*Parliament* was the elected government in England.)

Did Paul and the other men of the Long Room Club agree with this? No, they certainly did not. They were angry. American colonists didn't elect

any members to Parliament. So colonists really
had no say about passing new taxes. That wasn't
fair. Every colony had its own government. But
the local governments were not in charge of taxes.

In 1765, the Stamp Act was passed in England. Newspapers, contracts, marriage certificates, decks of cards, as well as many other paper goods now had to have a British stamp on them. Colonists had to pay for the stamp. Oh, did that get Paul Revere angry. He joined a secret group led by Sam Adams. It was called the Sons of Liberty. Paul designed a medal for all the members. They marched through Boston shouting, "Liberty! No stamps!"

The march worked, or so it seemed. News arrived from England: The Stamp Act was over.

In Boston, everyone celebrated. Fireworks burst in the night sky. Candles were lit in the windows of houses. A huge paper lantern stood in the center of town. Paul Revere may have designed the lantern himself.

It turned out, however, that people celebrated too soon. Two years later, in 1767, new taxes were announced on glass, paper, paint, and tea.

This made Paul and the other Sons of Liberty even angrier. They asked all the people of Boston to stop buying things from England. Then they went to the local government in Massachusetts. They convinced its members to send a letter to all the other colonies. The letter stated that what England was doing was wrong. If the colonists gave in to these taxes, more taxes were sure to follow. All the colonies needed to band together and stand up against England.

The king was furious when he found out about the letter. But ninety-two of the men in Boston who signed the letter stuck by it. In their honor, the Sons of Liberty had Paul make a big silver bowl. It is now in the Boston Museum of Fine Arts.

Did protests stop just because the king was angry?

No.

They continued.

British tax collectors arrived to collect the tax money. Paul and the other Sons of Liberty decided to rough them up. They waited until it was dark. Paul and his friends wore caps pulled low over their heads. And they blackened their faces. This way, the tax collectors couldn't identify their attackers.

After the fight, the British sent eight warships with cannons to Boston. They formed a semicircle around the harbor. It was a warning to the town that everyone had better behave.

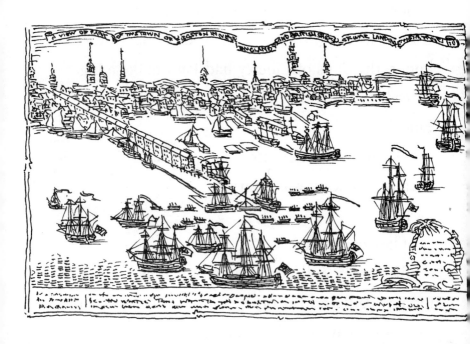

Paul made a copper engraving of the scene to spread the news of what happened. (Again, he made a copy of someone else's drawing.) Hundreds of people in Boston bought prints of it.

British soldiers became an unwelcome part of life in town. They had orders not to start fights with the people of Boston. But tempers were hot on both sides. Fighting was bound to come. It was just a question of when.

Chapter 5
Blood Is Spilled

For a year and a half, Boston stayed calm.
Then, on the snowy night of March 5, 1770,
everything changed. It is not completely clear
what started the clash. According to one account,
a British soldier didn't pay for repairs on a wig of

his. A young shop boy chased after him, and a fight started between the two. Very quickly, a crowd of townspeople gathered to defend the young boy. British troops rushed to the aid of the soldier. The fighting grew more serious. Then, all of a sudden, shots rang out. British soldiers were firing into the crowd! They were shooting colonists! A moment later, four men lay dead in the snow. Another man died four days later.

Paul Revere made an engraving of the event,
which became known as the Boston Massacre.
(A massacre is the murder of innocent people.)
Was Paul himself there, taking part in the fight?
Maybe. His engraving shows many details,

including exactly where the soldiers stood and where the bodies fell. So perhaps Paul was in the crowd. In any case, thousands of copies of his engraving were sold. It was in color. And what caught people's eyes were the red coats of the soldiers and the red blood of the victims. Because of the massacre, many more people now agreed with Paul and the Sons of Liberty. It was time to break free from England.

England saw that it had a huge problem on its hands. Parliament tried to calm down the colonists. The British soldiers were put on trial for the shootings. And the hated taxes were ended, all except for one. The tax on tea was left in place. It was a very small tax. But by this time, even a small tax on something cheap was too much for the Sons of Liberty to stand.

Three ships arrived from England carrying
chests full of tea. At the Green Dragon Tavern,
Paul took part in a meeting of the Sons of Liberty.

They decided to make sure that no one bought
the tea. And if no one bought the tea, no taxes
could be paid on it.

They came up with a secret plan. They were
going to hold a tea party—a very different kind
of tea party.

On the night of December 16, 1773, Paul
Revere and about 150 other men and boys sneaked
aboard the three ships. They had smeared their
faces with red paint and black soot. They wore
blankets over their shoulders. They were trying to
look like Indians. Paul Revere even gave himself
an Indian name. He called himself Mohawk. His
teenage son, Paul Jr., may also have been part of
the gang.

One by one, the chests were opened, and all
the tea—ten thousand pounds—was dumped
into Boston Harbor.

When the tea party was over, the Sons of Liberty marched to the State House. There was music and cheering from the crowd on the docks. Then the "Indians" went home to their families. But Paul Revere still had another job to do. Paul was chosen to spread the news about the Boston Tea Party. He was an excellent choice for the job. Paul was strong and never needed much sleep. He also loved riding horses. In fact, he owned a horse even though he did not need one for his silversmith business.

So off Paul Revere galloped to New York City and then to Philadelphia. In those days, it could take as long as nine days for a letter from Boston to reach New York City. But Paul would rise at dawn and ride hard and fast all day. It was winter, and roads were bad. Yet Paul Revere returned to Boston only eleven days later. And he brought back good news.

PAUL'S TRIP TO NEW YORK AND PHILADELPHIA

The Sons of Liberty in New York City and
Philadelphia were thrilled about the Boston Tea
Party. They would try to help the patriots in
Boston in every possible way. This was the first of
many important rides for Paul Revere. He became
a secret messenger for the cause of American
liberty. Because of him, people in other colonies

quickly learned about the important events taking place in Boston. The news that Paul delivered brought the colonies closer together. More and more, they were becoming united against a common enemy—the king of England.

Chapter 6
Creeping Up to War

So was Boston punished for its tea party?

Oh yes.

The king's warships closed the port of Boston. Until the tea was paid for, cargo ships couldn't come in or go out. Trading stopped. Soon, many businesses shut down. More British troops arrived to patrol the streets. Town meetings were banned. Rebels were to be sent to England for trial. Who spread word of all this terrible news to New York City and Philadelphia? Why, Paul Revere, of course.

It was dangerous work. Now people couldn't leave Boston without a pass. British soldiers knew Paul belonged to the Sons of Liberty. He was not going to be given any passes. So he had to sneak

out of town. Luck was usually on his side, and he managed to ride past British guards unnoticed. Paul Revere was not only a messenger—he also served as a spy for the Sons of Liberty. Years later, he wrote, "We held our meetings at the Green Dragon Tavern. We were so careful that our meetings should be kept secret." Paul's job was to find out what the British troops were up to. He wrote, "In the winter, towards spring, we frequently took turns, two and two, to watch the soldiers, by patrolling the streets all night."

He also kept a boat for snooping around Boston Harbor.

Once, British soldiers found him rowing right by Castle Island, the base for the British troops.

That time, Paul was not so lucky. The soldiers arrested him, and he spent three nights in jail.

Until 1774, each colony had looked out for its own interests. Now, the colonies did their best to help the people of Boston. Rice came in from South Carolina. Flour came from Maryland. Pennsylvania sent money. Even more important, the First Continental Congress—a group with representatives from every colony—met in Philadelphia to discuss what to do about the problems with England.

By mid-April, the Sons of Liberty were preparing for battle. A large number of guns and gunpowder were stored in the nearby town of Concord.

Sam Adams and John Hancock were about to travel to the Second Continental Congress. They were staying in Hancock's house in Lexington, a town only a few miles outside of Boston. By snooping around, Paul Revere learned that they were going to be arrested soon. Word had to get to Hancock and Adams about the danger they faced.

On April 18, Paul found out that the British were definitely up to something. One thousand British soldiers set out from Boston by boat. They crossed the Charles River to Charlestown. From there, they proceeded on foot to Lexington and Concord. They were ready for battle. Hancock and Adams had to be warned.

Paul Revere and a man named William Dawes were ready to sound the alarm to everyone in the countryside. Dawes set off on horseback.

WILLIAM DAWES

JOHN HANCOCK 1737–1793

JOHN HANCOCK

JOHN HANCOCK OWNED A SHIPPING BUSINESS AND WAS AMONG THE RICHEST MEN IN ALL OF THE THIRTEEN COLONIES. HE LOVED FINE CLOTHES, FANCY CHARIOTS, AND BIG MANSIONS. BUT HE ALSO SPENT HIS MONEY TO HELP THE CAUSE OF AMERICAN FREEDOM. HE WAS THE PRESIDENT OF THE SECOND CONTINENTAL CONGRESS WHEN THE DECLARATION OF INDEPENDENCE WAS WRITTEN, AND HIS SIGNATURE IS FAR BIGGER THAN ANYBODY ELSE'S. TODAY, WHEN PEOPLE ASK FOR YOUR "JOHN HANCOCK," IT MEANS THAT THEY WANT YOU TO SIGN SOMETHING.

John Hancock

SAMUEL ADAMS 1722–1803

BORN AND RAISED IN BOSTON, SAMUEL ADAMS WAS ONE OF THE FOUNDING FATHERS OF OUR COUNTRY. HE GRADUATED FROM HARVARD AND LATER WENT TO WORK IN THE FAMILY BREWERY. BUT HE WAS NEVER A SUCCESS IN BUSINESS. POLITICS WAS HIS REAL PASSION. HE BELIEVED—LONG BEFORE MOST OTHER PEOPLE DID—THAT THE COLONIES HAD TO BREAK AWAY FROM ENGLAND AND BECOME AN INDEPENDENT COUNTRY. ADAMS WAS A MEMBER OF THE FIRST CONTINENTAL CONGRESS. (FRIENDS BOUGHT HIM NEW CLOTHES AND PAID FOR HIS TRIP TO PHILADELPHIA.) HE, TOO, WAS A SIGNER OF THE DECLARATION OF INDEPENDENCE.

SAMUEL ADAMS

Paul was to take a different route. That way, if Dawes were caught and arrested, Paul still might be able to warn the people of Lexington and Concord.

Paul's first stop was Boston's Old North Church, the same church where he'd been a bell ringer as a boy. Its tall steeple could be seen in Charlestown. A few days before, he'd set up a clever plan. If the British were starting out by boat, two lanterns would be hung in the church steeple. If they were marching by land the whole way, there'd be only one lantern. The people in

Charlestown would then spread news of the British route to the towns that were farther away.

Troops had already been spotted setting out by ship from the harbor. Quickly, two lanterns were placed in the steeple. Then Paul raced home, where Rachel helped him into his boots and kissed him good-bye. He was in such a hurry that he forgot his spurs! According to stories Paul later told his grandchildren, the family dog also raced out of the house and followed Paul down to the waterfront. So Paul sent the dog back home with a note tied to its collar. The note asked Rachel to send his spurs. And that's exactly what the dog returned with! They were hanging around his neck.

Down at the waterfront, two friends were waiting by a boat that Paul had kept hidden all winter. The men were going to help Paul row across the harbor to Charlestown. A huge British warship was nearby. It was important to make as

little noise as possible. Paul had meant to bring
cloth to tie around the oars. But he'd forgotten
that, too. So one of the men raced to his
girlfriend's house. She offered one of her own
petticoats, which the men tore up and wrapped
around the oars.

That did the trick! The little rowboat passed
by the British ship in silence.

On the other side of the river in Charlestown, Paul was led to a horse. It was a strong, fast mare named Brown Beauty. He jumped in the saddle and off he headed for Lexington. It was the most important ride of his life.

Chapter 7
Oops!

From Charlestown, Paul galloped off in the
moonlight. He hadn't gotten far when he was

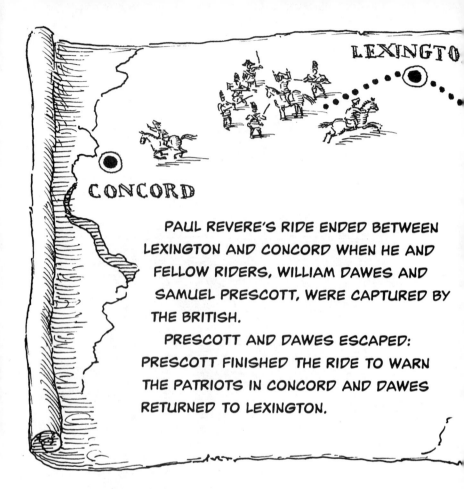

LEXINGTO

CONCORD

PAUL REVERE'S RIDE ENDED BETWEEN LEXINGTON AND CONCORD WHEN HE AND FELLOW RIDERS, WILLIAM DAWES AND SAMUEL PRESCOTT, WERE CAPTURED BY THE BRITISH.

PRESCOTT AND DAWES ESCAPED: PRESCOTT FINISHED THE RIDE TO WARN THE PATRIOTS IN CONCORD AND DAWES RETURNED TO LEXINGTON.

spotted by two British soldiers on horseback. But Paul managed to fly by them on Brown Beauty. On the way to Lexington, he kept stopping at houses, shouting to each family that the British were coming. Just before midnight, he rode into

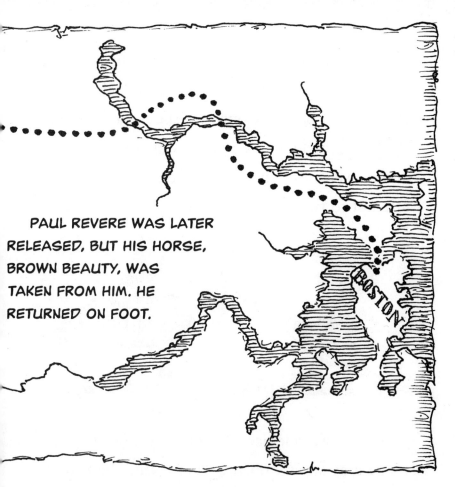

PAUL REVERE WAS LATER
RELEASED, BUT HIS HORSE,
BROWN BEAUTY, WAS
TAKEN FROM HIM. HE
RETURNED ON FOOT.

BOSTON

Lexington and reached Hancock and Adams.
Paul told them the grave news. One thousand
troops were coming for them, and then after that,
they were going to Concord to find all the hidden
weapons.

At this point, William Dawes met up with Paul Revere. After a little rest and a quick meal, they started out for Concord. About halfway there, Paul Revere's luck ran out. He was surrounded by about twelve British officers. One told him, "If you attempt to run . . . we will blow your brains out."

Dawes was luckier. He got away, but did not make it as far as Concord. As for Paul, he had to dismount. A British soldier led Brown Beauty away. Paul never saw the horse again.

Instead of arresting Paul, the soldiers rode off, leaving Paul alone in the road. They probably thought getting to Concord and fighting was more important than dealing with one prisoner. Paul returned on foot to Lexington, where he spent the night. He helped John Hancock and Sam Adams escape. But he never made it to Concord.

So what about Paul's ride made it so important?

Because of Paul Revere, the people of Lexington were prepared for the British troops. And indeed, the very next day, on April 19, the American Revolution began.

Nobody knows exactly who fired the first shot on Lexington Green. One British soldier was wounded and eight minutemen were left dead. (*Minutemen* was the name for local colonial soldiers because they would be ready to fight at a moment's notice.) The next day in Concord, however, five hundred minutemen managed to beat the British troops, who were forced to retreat to Boston. It was a victory for the colonists!

Paul did not take part in these first battles of the Revolutionary War. Once a real army was raised, he was no longer needed as a messenger. He hoped to become an important officer in the Continental Army. That didn't happen. He fought with local forces in Massachusetts and took part

in a sea battle in Castine, Maine. It ended in a terrible defeat for the Americans. Paul was in command of Boston soldiers on one of the ships. The British caught the ships by surprise in a rear attack. Some were destroyed. During the battle, Paul got separated from his troops. Their ship was destroyed. Paul and his men ended up walking all

the way back to Boston. At the time, Paul was accused of acting cowardly, but many years later his name was cleared.

Paul Revere was so good at so many things. But his time as a soldier was a low point in his life.

During the war, he made himself useful in other ways. He learned to make gunpowder. His powder mill kept American forces supplied with ammunition. The colonies now needed to print their own money. Who did the engravings for the new money? Paul Revere.

The war ended in 1781, and a new country was born. Paul Revere was now a citizen of the United States of America. He was forty-eight years old. Business at the silver shop was good. In time, he let his son take over. What did Paul do with the rest of his life? If you think he retired, you are very wrong!

REVERE TEAPOTS

OFTEN, A TEAPOT WAS AMONG THE MOST PRIZED ITEMS A FAMILY OWNED. THE BEST ONES WERE MADE OF SILVER AND COST A LOT OF MONEY. TEAPOTS MADE BY PAUL REVERE ARE STILL PRIZED TODAY. IN FACT, ONE OF HIS TEAPOTS WAS PRICED AT $798,500!

TEA WAS FIRST INTRODUCED TO THE PEOPLE OF EUROPE IN THE SEVENTEENTH CENTURY. SHIPS CAME BACK FROM CHINA WITH BAGS OF TEA LEAVES ON BOARD. IN ENGLAND, TEA BECAME VERY POPULAR VERY QUICKLY. PEOPLE DRANK IT MORNING, NOON, AND EVENING.

WHEN COLONISTS CAME FROM ENGLAND TO AMERICA, THEY CERTAINLY DIDN'T EXPECT TO STOP DRINKING TEA. SO THE TEA TRADE REMAINED STRONG. HOWEVER, COLONISTS COULD NOT SEND SHIPS TO BUY TEA FROM CHINA OR FROM ANY OTHER COUNTRY WHERE TEA GREW. THEY HAD TO BUY IT FROM BRITISH TRADERS WHO DECIDED THE PRICE.

Chapter 8
United States Citizen

Paul had always been a sharp businessman. Now that the war was over, he saw that there were many interesting opportunities for Americans.

For example, before the war, iron tools and machines had to be bought from England. The colonists couldn't make them themselves. This wasn't the case anymore.

Paul decided to open a foundry, a shop that made things out of cast iron. Soon he was turning out hammers, anvils, stoves, and more. He had always loved church bells, and many of the ones in Boston were old and cracked. So Paul taught himself how to make and repair bells. He made hundreds of bells, some as big as the ones in Old North Church. Young boys liked to come and watch the work. Paul enjoyed the company, but he had to keep warning the boys about staying away from the hammers and fire. "Take care, boys," he'd say. "If that hammer should hit your head, you'd ring louder than these bells do." Many of the bells made at Paul Revere's foundry are still ringing in Boston churches.

The United States was building ships for its brand-new Navy. The foundry turned out nails, spikes, rudders, and bolts for the Navy. Ships were mostly made of wood, but ship bottoms needed to be covered with a sheet of copper. (Wood would rot too quickly.) Before the war, all the copper sheeting had to come from England. Not anymore. So Paul learned all about how thin sheets of copper were made. Then he spent nearly all the money he had to build a copper mill.

COPPER WORKS

MASSACHUSETTS STATE HOUSE

He was in his sixties by then, but still willing to take a gamble. Paul's copper sheeting was so good, it was not only used on ships. The copper skin on the dome of the Massachusetts State House and New York City's City Hall came from Paul's mill. The Revere Copper company is still in business today.

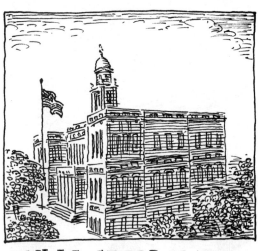

NYC CITY HALL

Although not rich, Paul and Rachel were
well-off. In 1800, they sold their house on North
Square and moved into a bigger brick house in
Boston that they'd bought. They also had a small

house in Canton, a country town near the copper mill. Paul still enjoyed saddling up a horse and dashing off for a ride.

PAUL REVERE'S PROPERTY

After Rachel died in 1813, Paul spent most of his time in Canton with his growing family. He was an old man now. And while most men wore

IN CANTON, MASSACHUSETTS

long trousers and hats with brims, Paul still favored three-cornered hats and knee britches. He looked like someone from the past.

By the time he died at eighty-three on May 10, 1818, he had more than fifty grandchildren. They had always enjoyed hearing about their grandpa's daring ride. But with each passing year, there were fewer people outside the Revere family who remembered it.

Chapter 9
Fame at Last!

Fifty years after Paul Revere's death, the Revere silver company was still in business. But outside of his family, no one remembered Paul Revere. That all changed in 1861. Why did Paul Revere suddenly become famous?

It was all because of a poem.

Henry Wadsworth Longfellow was the best-loved poet in America. He was known for writing about America's past. He wrote about the Pilgrims in a poem called "The Courtship of Miles Standish." He wrote about Native Americans in "Hiawatha." In 1861, he wrote "Paul Revere's Ride." It turned Paul into a folk hero.

The poem starts off with the lines:
  Listen my children and you shall hear
  Of the midnight ride of Paul Revere.

PAUL REVERE.
BORN
IN BOSTON,
JANUARY, 1734:
DIED
MAY, 1818.

Longfellow's poem describes Paul's ride as a thrilling adventure. Paul barely escapes from the British soldiers. But he manages to reach Sam Adams and John Hancock. He warns them that their lives are in danger. Thanks to Paul, they remain safe.

As far as the real ride of Paul Revere, Longfellow got many of the details wrong. He had read Paul's own account of the ride. So he knew what the facts were. Yet he decided to change some things, anyway. Perhaps one reason was to make the ride more exciting for readers. For instance, in the poem, Paul is all alone the whole time. That wasn't so. Longfellow also left out certain things. For example, he never says that Paul was stopped by British soldiers.

Longfellow wanted to depict Paul Revere as a brave man doing his best for the cause of freedom. His poem was about the beginning of the American Revolution. It came out at a

time when the United States was about to go
to war again.

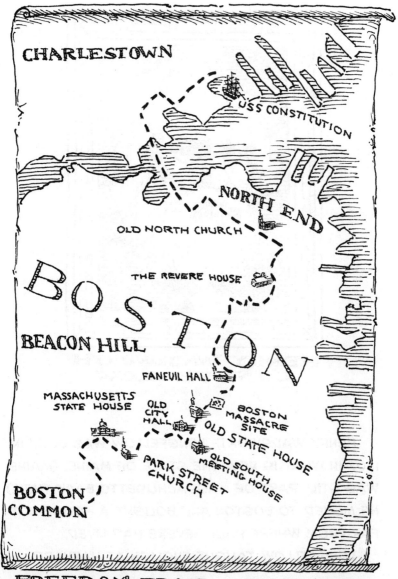

FREEDOM TRAIL, BOSTON

HENRY WADSWORTH LONGFELLOW 1807–1882

HENRY WADSWORTH
LONGFELLOW

HENRY WADSWORTH LONGFELLOW WAS BORN IN
1807 IN WHAT IS NOW THE STATE OF MAINE. (MAINE
WAS STILL PART OF MASSACHUSETTS BACK THEN.)
HE MOVED TO BOSTON AND BOUGHT A HOUSE NOT
FAR FROM WHERE PAUL REVERE HAD LIVED.

LONGFELLOW TAUGHT ENGLISH AT HARVARD

COLLEGE FOR MANY YEARS. BUT IN 1854, HE STOPPED TEACHING TO WRITE FULL-TIME. HE SOON BECAME THE MOST FAMOUS POET IN THE UNITED STATES. HE WAS PROBABLY THE RICHEST ONE, TOO. BY 1874 HE WAS GETTING PAID AS MUCH AS THREE THOUSAND DOLLARS FOR ONE POEM. THAT WAS A SMALL FORTUNE BACK THEN.

LONGFELLOW WAS VERY INTERESTED IN THE POLITICS OF THE DAY. LIKE MANY PEOPLE IN THE NORTH, HE BELIEVED SLAVERY WAS WRONG. IT HAD TO BE ABOLISHED, MEANING ENDED. HE WROTE A BOOK OF POEMS ABOUT THE EVILS OF SLAVERY. HE ALSO GAVE MONEY TO HELP SLAVES ESCAPE TO FREEDOM IN THE NORTH.

IN 1861, "PAUL REVERE'S RIDE" APPEARED IN A POPULAR MAGAZINE CALLED *THE ATLANTIC MONTHLY*. TWENTY-FIVE THOUSAND COPIES WERE SOLD ALMOST RIGHT AWAY!

In April 1861, the Civil War started between the North and South. It was a war over slavery, which was still legal in the South.

In "Paul Revere's Ride," Longfellow was trying to make a point about the Civil War. He was saying that the North had to fight to end slavery. It was a war for freedom, just as the Revolutionary War had been.

"Paul Revere's Ride" became so popular that for decades all schoolchildren read it. Some learned all the lines by heart. Today, many critics think it isn't a very good poem. But it touched American readers of the time. Paul Revere became a famous patriot. Music was composed about the midnight ride. Famous artists did paintings of Paul on his horse. Books were written about him. Towns were named after him, not only in New England, but also in Pennsylvania, Minnesota, and Missouri.

His three-story house still stands. It is known

as the Revere House. Lots of school groups and tourists visit it every year.

In Boston's North End, the Revere House is the only building from colonial times that remains. Nearby is a large bronze statue of Paul Revere.

He is on horseback and caught midgallop. His coattails are flying. He is bringing important news—news that will change the history of America.

TIMELINE OF
PAUL REVERE'S LIFE

1734	Paul Revere is born in Boston
1741	Paul starts at North Writing School
1754	After his father's death, Paul takes over the silver shop
1755	Paul goes off to fight in the French and Indian War
1757	Paul marries Sara (Sary) Orne
1758	The Reveres' first child, Deborah, is born
1765	The Stamp Act is passed by British Parliament
1770	The Boston Massacre takes place on March 5
1773	Paul takes part in the Boston Tea Party on December 16 Paul begins serving as a messenger and spy for the Sons of Liberty After Sary's death, Paul marries Rachel Walker
1775	Paul sets off for Lexington, MA, on April 18 to warn of oncoming British troops On April 19, the Battle of Lexington and Concord mark the beginning of the American Revolution
1781	Paul returns to a private life
1800	Paul opens a copper sheeting mill
1813	Rachel, Paul's second wife, dies
1818	Paul dies
1861	Henry Wadsworth Longfellow publishes the poem "Paul Revere's Ride"

TIMELINE OF
THE WORLD

George Washington is born — **1732**

Danish explorer Vitus Bering discovers Alaska — **1741**

George III becomes king of England — **1760**

First Continental Congress meets in Philadelphia — **1774**

The Declaration of Independence is signed on July 4 — **1776**

James Cook discovers Hawaii — **1778**

Great Britain recognizes the United States of America
as a separate country — **1783**

US Constitution is drafted in Philadelphia — **1787**

French Revolution begins;
soon there are executions of French aristocrats — **1789**

Construction of the White House begins — **1792**

Noah Webster's first American dictionary is published — **1806**

Abraham Lincoln is born — **1809**

War of 1812 between the US and Great Britain begins — **1812**

US wins the War of 1812 — **1815**

Civil War starts — **1861**

Bibliography

Fischer, David Hackett. **Paul Revere's Ride.** Oxford University Press, New York, 1994.

Forbes, Esther. **Paul Revere and the World He Lived In.** Mariner Books, New York, 1942.

* Fritz, Jean. **And Then What Happened, Paul Revere?** G. P. Putnam's Sons, New York, 1973.

* Giblin, James Cross. **The Many Rides of Paul Revere.** Scholastic Press, New York, 2007.

* McGovern, Ann. **If You Lived in Colonial Times.** Scholastic, New York, 1985.

Miller, Joel J. **The Revolutionary Paul Revere.** Thomas Nelson, Nashville, 2010.

* Stevenson, Augusta. **Paul Revere: Boston Patriot.** Aladdin Paperbacks, New York, 1946.

* Starred books are for young readers